PLANT PARTS

Why Do

Ste

Celeste Bishop

PowerKiDS press.

New York

Published in 2016 by The Rosen Publishing Group, Inc.
29 East 21st Street, New York, NY 10010

First Edition

Editor: Sarah Machajewski
Book Design: Mickey Harmon

Photo Credits: Cover (plant) stockphoto mania/Shutterstock.com; cover, p. 1 (logo, frame) Perfect Vectors/Shutterstock.com; cover, pp. 1, 3–4, 7–8, 11–12, 15–16, 19–20, 23–24 (background) djgis/Shutterstock.com; p. 5 Bildagentur Zoonar GmbH/Shutterstock.com; p. 6 Kim Doucette/Shutterstock.com; pp. 9, 13–14 (sky) Nemeziya/Shutterstock.com; pp. 9–10, 13 (plant) ifong/Shutterstock.com; p. 10 (sky) Galina Gutarin/Shutterstock.com; p. 14 (asparagus) Krasowit/Shutterstock.com; p. 17 Przemyslaw Wasilewski/Shutterstock.comp. 18 Denis and Yulia Pogostins/Shutterstock.com; p. 21 Veniamin Kraskov/Shutterstock.com; p. 22 sumroeng chinnapan/Shutterstock.com.

Library of Congress Cataloging-in-Publication Data

Bishop, Celeste, author.
 Why do plants have stems? / Celeste Bishop.
    pages cm. — (Plant parts)
 Includes index.
ISBN 978-1-5081-4233-1 (pbk.)
ISBN 978-1-5081-4234-8 (6 pack)
ISBN 978-1-4994-1851-4 (library binding)
1. Stems (Botany)—Juvenile literature. 2. Plants—Juvenile literature. I. Title.
QK646.B57 2016
575.4—dc23
                              2015021406

Manufactured in the United States of America

CPSIA Compliance Information: Batch #BW16PK: For Further Information contact Rosen Publishing, New York, New York at 1-800-237-9932

Contents

What Do Stems Do?   4

It's All Connected   8

Carrying Water and Matter   11

Many Kinds of Stems   15

Higher Plants   20

Words to Know   24

Index   24

Websites   24

Stems are an important plant part. Do you know what they do?

Stems help a plant stand up.

Stems are connected to **roots** and **leaves**.

stem

leaves

roots

Roots take in water. Then, the stem carries water to the leaves.

Roots also take in nutrients. Nutrients are tiny pieces of matter. The stem carries them to the leaves.

nutrients

There are many kinds of stems.
Green plants have soft stems.

Tree trunks are another kind of stem! They're tough and woody.

Some stems grow under the ground. They're called **tubers**. A potato is a tuber.

Not all plants have stems.
Plants with stems are called
higher plants.

Can you see why stems are important?

Words to Know

leaves

roots

tubers

Index

N
nutrients, 12, 13

T
tubers, 19

R
roots, 8, 9, 11, 12

W
water, 11

Websites

Due to the changing nature of Internet links, PowerKids Press has developed an online list of websites related to the subject of this book. This site is updated regularly. Please use this link to access the list: www.powerkidslinks.com/part/stem